RESURRECTION FREEDOM

God's Power to Face Life's Challenges

RESURRECTION FREEDOM

God's Power to Face Life's Challenges

REV. DR. GREGORY SELTZ

Rev. Dr. Gregory Seltz is the Executive Director of LCRL, the Lutheran Center for Religious Liberty. He serves as a talented speaker, writer, and preacher on topics such as Church and State, Two-Kingdoms – One Mission, Evangelism, Missions, and Cross-Cultural Ministry. In Resurrection Freedom, he will talk about what holds you in the crisis of life, the blessings of life and the hope of what life is all about.

Washington, D.C.

ISBN-13: 978-0-692-11968-6

Printed in the United States of America

CONTENTS

INTRODUCTION

And the truth shall set you free!

There are many definitions of truth in our world today. From "alternate facts" to "fake news," it's easy to get confused, wondering where to turn for real truth, the truth that will ultimately set us free.

The answer is found in John 8:32 where Jesus Christ tells His followers that "If you abide in My word, you are truly My disciples, and you will know the truth, and the truth will set you free."

Freedom from what, you ask? Freedom from the bondage of sin that would lead to eternal destruction. Christ came as God's very own Son to be born both God and man, to live the life of perfection we could not, and to take the weight of punishment for our sins to death on the cross. The very resurrection that brought forth Jesus from death to life now gives all believers in Him the freedom to live as redeemed children of God.

The impact of Resurrection Freedom on life is what you will find throughout these chapters, all of which are excerpts from **The Lutheran Hour**®, prepared and delivered by the Rev. Dr. Gregory Seltz, Speaker of The Lutheran Hour. Taken from real life, these messages relay how brand-new life in Christ is an invitation to a brand-new start. Whether you are broken or whole, a lifelong Christian or one newly seeking the truth, this book is for you!

Real life. Real freedom.

This truth will set you free!

CHAPTER ONE

REPENTANCE REFRESHMENT

Acts 3:18-21

In 2005 a store opened in the Mall of America, in Minneapolis, Minnesota. It was called MinneNAPolis—that's right, MinneNAPolis. Its purpose? To offer "rest to shoppers." It rented comfy spots where weary shoppers could take naps for 70 cents a minute. Founded by PowerNap Sleep Centers of Boca Raton, Florida, the store included themed rooms such as Asian Mist, Tropical Isle, and Deep Space, and the walls were thick enough to drown out the sounds of squealing children or bustling shoppers.

The company's website featured these descriptions: "Escape the pressures of the real world into the pleasures of an ideal one." "It's not just napping—some guests will want to listen to music, put their feet up, watch the water trickling in the beautiful stone waterfall, breathe in the positive-ionization-filled air, enjoy the full-body massager, and just take an enjoyable escape from their fast-paced lifestyle."

My first reaction was, "Do you mean that we now need to take a rest from our shopping, too?" I thought shopping was supposed to be the respite from the workaday world. Wow! It seems that even our leisure activities are tiring us out today! But the real-life reality is that what we need isn't an escape into an ideal, utopian world. No, what we need is real refreshment in the middle of our very real lives, just as they are.

It seems that real refreshment continues to be the one thing that eludes us today, and there's good reason for it. In today's text,

St. Peter, a disciple of Jesus, speaks about "times of refreshing" that come—not from our creations, our escapes, or our best efforts—but from a repentance and a returning to God by faith. There are certain things that will never be right in our hearts and minds until we are reconciled with the Lord who created and redeemed us.

In fact, when Peter is speaking to the audience of the Israelites, he reminds them that God has been in the business of humanity's salvation from the very beginning of time. Without God, nothing in this world can satisfy us or grant us restorative peace. God's offer of grace is not a temporary suspension of this life's tragedies and travails. No, it is an offer of Christ's eternal life in the midst of life's realities, refreshment in His Name in the midst of life's challenges, and resurrection life as His sure promise to all who believe.

St. Peter called the people of that day, just as he calls you and me today, to repent and return to God for the forgiveness of sins. He invited a faith relationship with the Messiah Jesus for times of refreshment resourced by God, as only His grace can provide. Peter says, "This is how God fulfilled what He had foretold through all the prophets, saying that His Messiah would suffer. Repent, then, and turn to God, so that your sins may be wiped out, and times of refreshing may come from the Lord."

This call for repentant refreshment comes amidst a tumultuous public event where things were spiraling out of control for Peter and John. They were confronted by a lame man begging near the temple. That wasn't unusual; beggars often lived off the benevolence of templegoers. And so this man approaches Peter and John for money, for what he thought he needed. But what he got instead was a healing of body and soul. Peter's message to the man and to all who listened was this: We don't have gold or silver, but what we have is more precious—the Name of Jesus, yours as a gift.

In this case, the Name came with a very public healing—one that had people thinking of Peter and John as having some special powers or blessings of their own. But Peter would have none of that.

His message was about the Name of Jesus, the blessing of Jesus. This healing was merely another way to proclaim God's greater blessings of forgiveness, life, salvation, and eternal refreshment for all who believe in Christ, the Messiah, their Savior.

Repentant refreshment? That's what Peter sought to deliver that day. And that's what he is offering to you and to me this day.

But why? Why do we need to get so spiritual about this? If we're overwhelmed, or tired (and a lot of us are today), I thought we just needed leisure time, time off, or a little more sleep. Don't we just need to work less and enjoy more entertainment and R&R? Don't we just need a spiritual power nap once in a while in order to get the kind of refreshment we crave for body, mind, and spirit?

I guess it depends on what kind of things are making us weary. If we're merely overly tired or in need of some extra energy, then, yes, a power nap or some well-needed exercise might do. But what if we're dealing with things that simply cannot be solved with a little shut-eye? What if we're dealing with an issue that remains despite our best efforts? I'm talking about the things that keep us up at night, the things that no amount of money in the bank can fix—things deep in our hearts, always on our minds, an inevitable drumbeat of missed opportunities or deep-seated disappointments!

Repentant refreshment deals with these very issues—issues where there is an eternal, just payment due. It takes these issues to the cross where Jesus the Messiah took upon Himself the weariness-causing sin, the strength-sapping failures, and every rebellion that exists in every one of our lives, and literally blotted them out by His death on the cross—a suffering Savior for real refreshment.

Peter uses a common image to the people of his day when He says that God blotted out their transgressions through Jesus. Debts of that day were written—literally carved into wax tablets—where they would remain clear until each debt was paid. To blot them out was to take an object and literally scratch them away as if they never existed!

In the Old Testament, King David knew the bone-aching power

of unrepentance and the healing refreshment of God's grace. Consider the story of David and Bathsheba. It's a brutal reminder that David's temptations are ours, and that those kinds of lusts and sins and debauchery are the very things that not only destroy our relationship to God and to one another, they destroy us as well. Listen to how David talks about such things in Psalm 32:

> "Blessed is the one whose transgressions are forgiven, whose sins are covered. Blessed is the one whose sin the Lord does not count against them and in whose spirit is no deceit. When I kept silent, my bones wasted away through my groaning all day long. For day and night Your hand was heavy on me; my strength was sapped as if in the heat of summer. Then I acknowledged my sin to You. I did not cover up my iniquity. I said, 'I will confess my transgressions to the Lord.' And You forgave the guilt of my sin."

Blotted out. We need more than a power nap, more than a little of God's help for today. Peter is proclaiming God's offer of real forgiveness for sin and eternal guilt; God's offer of a resurrection life for people destined for self-induced destruction; a message where even the blessings of this life are merely a foretaste of eternal life with Him.

The message of the Bible is clear: Repent of your sins, of your desire to be the one in total control of your life. Believe in the One who created you, redeemed you, and yearns to reconcile you with Himself so that you will be refreshed by His grace, confident of His love, and empowered by His Spirit.

Peter says, "Repent, then, and turn to God, so that your sins may be wiped out, that times of refreshing may come from the Lord, and that He may send the Messiah, who has been appointed for you—even Jesus."

Now, some of you may be thinking, "So if repentance is the way to godly refreshment, then how does this repentance thing work?" Well, the first thing that comes with repentance is that God, by the power of His Spirit through His Law, brings you to the knowledge and belief that your life is not what it should be, and that remaining on the path of your spiritual indifference—or worse, your self-righteous solution— is the way to certain death and eternal destruction.

By the power of God's Spirit, see the weight and emotionally draining power of sin, guilt, and worry in your life as something to be repented of, sorrowed over, even turned away from. Repentance is a call to turn away from our ill-fated attempts to live life on our terms. It is a call to sorrow and contrition for those things that dishonor the God of heaven who made us and redeemed us. It is a call to realize the depth of despair from which we have been rescued.

Do you remember the opening scenes of *The Wide World of Sports* television program from the 1970s? I can still hear the words "the thrill of victory; the agony of defeat." While hearing "the agony of defeat," we saw footage of a man cascading off a ski jump, rocketing out of control off the end of the ramp, tumbling and flipping wildly, and crashing through a fence, finally coming to rest before a crowd of stunned spectators. This leads to the question: Did he fall or did he abort the jump? Was this merely another athlete messing up, or was this an athlete boldly changing course?

What viewers didn't realize was that he chose to fall rather than finish the jump. Why? As he explained later, the jump surface had become too fast and midway down the ramp he realized that if he completed the jump he would land beyond the safe landing area, which could have been fatal. Halting the jump literally saved his life.

To change one's course in life can be a dramatic and sometimes painful undertaking, but change is better than a fatal landing at the end. Repentance is seeing clearly that a path without God clearly ends in death and despair. Repentance is the power of the Spirit of God in action, turning us away from such a life and turning us to God by faith.

Later, in Acts chapter 5, Peter says that "God exalted Jesus to His own right hand as Prince and Savior that He might give repentance and forgiveness of sins."

It's clear. Our real problem is not our productivity or amount of leisure; it's not about how much money we have, or how much time we need. The world is a hard and unrelenting place because it is evil. This world has pain because there is sin. The great challenge in a life of abundant refreshment is the rebellion that lives in every human heart which leads to separation from God.

The key to times of refreshment is our relationship to God. The real key to repentant refreshment is faith in the Jesus who makes such repentance possible and blesses us with forgiveness and abundant life lived in the power of His Spirit! Faith in Him is key because now we have a merciful place to stand before God, without fear and without judgment—a place of hope in Christ, a place that is sure and certain, a place in God's presence, the One who is the author, the sustainer, indeed the refresher, of all of life.

Sin disconnects a person from God. Sin literally removes us from that fount of refreshment, that living water that you and I so desperately need. Repentance, by the power of the Holy Spirit, reconnects us to God because it turns us away from ourselves and shows us indeed what we are missing. But even more wonderfully, it returns us to the One who not only created us, but redeemed us by His grace. And the returns on that grace just keep on coming, don't they?

Not only did the man healed in Acts 3 have a new, hope-filled standing before the Lord, he was now able to take his stand—to take his place—in the temple as one praising and worshipping God. He was not only healed, he was returned to society in ways that only his healing from the Lord could effect. He was reconnected to others because he was reconciled to God in the Name of Jesus.

When repentant refreshment is poured into our lives, it turns us away from our selfish, self-centered struggle to take control of our lives. Repentant refreshment comes from being immersed in God's

Word and the deep well of His Living Water, being refreshed by His Spirit-filled promises, and His clear proclamation of grace. When we are refreshed in Him, we are empowered to be His people to others, vessels of His grace.

So, today, let God's continual repentance refreshment strengthen your ability to stand not only by grace in His presence, but to continue to take your stand in love in the lives of those you care about. And don't let anything other than the grace of Jesus motivate you to care for others. For as Peter and John learned, even when you share Jesus, a bit of chaos can ensue. But think about it! Christ's blessings can be shared and received even in the middle of chaos!

Justice Thurgood Marshall shared the following wise story. There were two unmarried sisters who had such a bitter fight that they stopped speaking to one another. Unable or unwilling to leave their small home, they continued to use the same rooms and sleep in the same bedroom. A chalk line divided the sleeping area into two halves. Chalk divided every room so that each sister could come and go and get her own meals without trespassing on the other sister's space. In the black of night, each could hear the breathing and snoring of the other. For years, they co-existed in grinding silence. Neither was willing to take the first step to reconciliation, let alone refreshment in their relationship.

Then one night, a sister got up to go to the bathroom and fell, breaking her hip. The other sister, awakened by the fall and the scream of pain, jumped out of bed and crossed the chalk line, coming to her sister's side. Even though she couldn't resist delivering a jab as to why her sister would do such a foolish thing as to trip over her own feet, the sister who crossed the line held onto her foe of the past few years until the paramedics came and carried her to the hospital.

Supreme Court Justice Thurgood Marshall added these words at the end: "The legal system can force open doors and sometimes knock down walls, but it cannot build bridges." Marshall was right. That is the job of Christ and His church—repentant refreshment in action.

It took real pain to finally get this sister to look to her sibling with begrudged mercy. But that's not what it means to be God's people. God's people know that Jesus erased the lines between us and God, lines that we selfishly drew. Christians know that Jesus doesn't just erase the lines—He willingly, not begrudgingly—crosses them, bringing His mercy, His continued care, and His abundant life to us as a gift. Christians know that all these blessings were meant to be shared whenever and wherever He so desires, and that's what Peter and John were doing that day.

Peter called his brothers to faith by calling them to repentance and pointing them to Jesus as their Savior. And when you know Him in repentant faith, you know the forgiveness, the love, and the mercy that only He can provide. When you know Him, real refreshment is possible because in Him your relationship to God is renewed again.

So, when all the machinations of modern life fail to bring the refreshment we need; when leisure is not enough; when work is not enough; even when the things of this world that we love are not enough, the call to faith in Jesus Christ remains. In Him, sin is forgiven. In Him, life with God is restored. In Him, we are reconciled to God with a firm place to stand graced in His Presence. With Him, there is a refreshment of soul that affects even the body. Just ask a lame man who was healed one day by the word of an apostle who blessed Him in Jesus' Name.

Resurrection Reflections

1. What new insights did the Holy Spirit bring to your mind and heart as you read this chapter?

2. Repentance involves turning away from our sin toward God. Think of the ski jumper who aborted his jump to avoid injury or possible death. What sins are you struggling with today that need a course correction?

3. Think of King David before and after his confession of sin and repentance. What might refreshment look like for you after repenting of your sin?

4. What could be different tomorrow if you repented today? What, if any, are the obstacles standing in the way of your refreshment repentance?

5. The ultimate gift of refreshment is the forgiveness that is ours through Christ's death and resurrection. How does knowing that God has forgiven you influence how you live each day?

CHAPTER TWO

HUMBLE STRENGTH
FOR ETERNAL SALVATION

Philippians 2:5-11

Palm Sunday is a very special day for Christians. It always occurs the Sunday before Easter and inaugurates the week of our Lord's Passion, His entering into Jerusalem for the final time before being arrested, sentenced to death, crucified on the cross on Good Friday, and raised from the dead on the day we call Easter. While Palm Sunday is a great Sunday for the Christian, it also begins a week of retracing the tumultuous events that His followers encountered. It is a record of events like none other in human history. What happened to Jesus Christ in this week literally changed the world. The benefits of what Jesus Christ endured and accomplished during this week of His passion continues to change people's lives today!

Someone long ago coined the phrase "It's a dog-eat-dog world." So what does that adage imply? That human beings can be ruthlessly competitive! Many people will spare no expense in destroying one another just to get ahead. It's a "survival of fittest" kind of mentality.

I have a friend who recently backed this up, who now works in one of our Lutheran organizations. He said, "I used to work in the corporate world, but I really like it here. In my last job, a major corporation here in the United States, the competition was fierce. It was high stress ALL the time. But here, well, everyone is kind. Also, you feel like you're working for something much more important. There are things in this job that make it clear that it's now about more than just making the next buck!"[1]

If you are a Christian, you might relate to that sentiment. It can be hard to be a Christian and work for a business with bosses and managers who seemingly only care about the company's bottom line. That's what makes Jesus and Palm Sunday so important to appreciate. A Bible text often read on Palm Sunday is from Philippians, chapter two. This book was a letter to a group of Christians in Philippi, an encouraging letter that St. Paul wrote to a people, most of whom were Roman citizens. He wrote this letter because he knew that the Christian faith of the Philippians would be opposed by the forces of the world and by someone else's bottom line. Hardship would come to them. In fact, Paul was writing this letter when he himself was under house arrest due to unjust allegations. Nevertheless, Paul endured.

Consider how Paul begins this letter: "Have this mind among yourselves, which is yours in Christ Jesus, who, though He was in the form of God, did not count equality with God a thing to be grasped, but emptied Himself, by taking the form of a servant, being born in the likeness of men" (Philippians 2:5-7). He begins by speaking of humility.

In the movie *Sully*, US Airways pilot Chesley Sullenberger successfully made a water landing after a flock of birds flew into both engines of his airliner at only 2,800 feet, shortly after takeoff. A total of 155 souls were on board and, miraculously, every one of them survived. The world soon called it the "Miracle on the Hudson." In this box office hit that mirrored this true-to-life story of heroism, Sully is praised for being the "X factor" in the equation. But in all humility, he disagreed. He pointed to the co-pilot and flight attendants onboard. He mentioned the United States Coast Guard, the police, and all first responders as he said, "We all did our job. We survived."[2] The captain, the consummate picture of humility. The world, though, still remembers just one name—Sully.

On Palm Sunday Jesus rode into Jerusalem as a hero. The Israelites who cheered Him on that morning believed He was their great Messiah and Redeemer. Some believed that Jesus was about to inaugurate a new age and liberate their nation as had not been seen since the days of Moses and King David. They recalled their former glory, when Israel was duly respected and revered.

That is not what Paul shares with us, though, in this passage from Philippians. Paul echoes the joy that is ours in a Savior who comes to His people with great humility as he writes "Who, though He was in the form of God, did not count equality with God a thing to be grasped, but emptied Himself, by taking the form of a servant, being born in the likeness of men." For the world in which we live and for the world in which Paul and the Philippians lived, this was the kind of hero that was needed—God-ordained. As Paul was inspired to encourage the Philippians, even now he encourages us: "Have this same mind among yourselves, which is yours in Christ Jesus."

Who was Jesus and what was His mindset? We learn of this in the first verses of Philippians 2: "Do nothing out of selfish ambition; in humility count others more significant than yourselves; look not only to your own interests, but also to the interest of others" (vs. 2-4). That was Jesus. On Palm Sunday He came to Jerusalem, not to destroy the Romans and set up an earthly rule never seen before, but to destroy something more significant: the sin that had threatened to forever destroy the relationship between God and mankind. Jesus did not ride into Jerusalem on Palm Sunday on the biggest steed, a conquering hero of glitz and glamour. No; He rode into town in humble fashion, on a donkey—a colt, the foal of a donkey. While the crowds were loud and their praise intense, He came in more or less quietly.

In medieval times, many sons of great kings (as was also true in ancient times) tried to outdo the ways of their fathers. If the father had been an oppressive king, the son became ruthless. If the father beat with a whip, the son would scourge with scorpions.

The desire for power and control overcame them. King Ahab, King Ahaz, and even David's sons feuded, killed, and caused harm. These and countless others whose biographies litter the annals of history destroyed people to gain and retain power. However, we are reminded on Palm Sunday that King Jesus, "though He was in the form of God, did not count equality with God a thing to be grasped, but emptied Himself, by taking the form of a servant" (vs. 6-7).

When it may seem like you must commit treason against your conscience in order to make a mark in this world, Jesus delivers a better, more perfect way—freedom from tyranny and oppression. My friends, across the vast lands of this planet, human beings still wage war against others for the sake of power and prestige. But this should not be so among you who are Christ's people. Jesus, the King of the world, King for ALL time, emptied Himself, set aside His power for "a time" in order to become a lowly servant, to become the very Lamb of God who alone would take away the sin, guilt, and shame of the world—even the power of death—as shared by Paul in verse 8: "And being found in human form, He humbled Himself by becoming obedient to the point of death, even death on a cross."

When you stop to think about favorite leaders you've encountered, I'm guessing that those you recall have been or are people of great influence and ability—people who regularly took time out to be a blessing to you. It was once said of President Abraham Lincoln that whenever he spoke with others, he made them feel like they were president. Such people are strong in humility. Their power isn't in might, or power, or prestige. Their mindset is one of encouragement and the lifting up of others.

Jesus was just like that ... but, oh, so much more and better. Over and over again, in the Bible books of Matthew, Mark, Luke, and John, we hear how Jesus was a friend of sinners and the downtrodden. He connected with them. He loved them. He ate and drank with them. He lifted them up; He made them His own. Jesus came to earth to serve people.

The Bible proclaims Jesus to be God's Son—the very highest priest, the greatest son a king like King David could ever imagine, the heir of David promised for centuries after David died, and the one for whom the world waited in great expectation. Man, we're talking about supreme royalty here! Yet then He laid it all down. He set it all aside for a time so that He could become the Lamb of God who takes away the sin of the world. Why? Because there was nothing that any imposter-ruler could try to take away from Him. When God the Father calls you His one and only Son, you are golden.

Paul writes this in Philippians 2:9-11: "Therefore God has highly exalted Him and bestowed on Him the Name that is above every name, so that at the Name of Jesus every knee should bow, in heaven and on earth and under the earth, and every tongue confess that Jesus Christ is Lord, to the glory of God the Father." Jesus, being the Son of God, the Father's one and only perfect Son, laid down His life, not just because He would be raised again, but because His sacrifice on the cross could destroy the power of sin and death in this world.

Yes, there is still sin in the world. Yes, there are still people who lack humility; ruthless people still command destructive wars that cause great harm and lay hold of others, violently and mercilessly. But their ability to cause hurt is only for this day and age.

My friends, there is a whole eternity that awaits us. As the apostle Peter writes, "But you are a chosen people, a royal priesthood, a holy nation, a people belonging to God" (1 Peter 2:9). Nobody—no ruthless leader, no unjust manager, no vengeful neighbor, no CEO on a power trip—can ever take that away from you. Nor can they dissuade you from being a blessing to those around you.

You live for something bigger and greater than any other can ever try to promise on this earth. You are Kingdom people, whose King is none other than Christ the Lord. Your greatest work will always be heroic, when through your life you graciously and humbly point others to the Christ, whose Name all tongues will one day confess to the glory of God the Father.

Resurrection Reflections

1. What new insights did the Holy Spirit bring to your mind and heart as you read this chapter?

2. What is the driver behind a "survival of the fittest" mindset? What rests at the core of "putting the needs of others first"? Where do you fall along this spectrum?

3. Humble or strong—which would you rather be? Why or why not? How was Christ Jesus both?

4. What is the result of Jesus' humiliation for our sake? What is the result of His strength? Are they different or the same?

5. How might you become more of a servant to others?

CHAPTER THREE

COUNT ON CHRIST'S MERCY FOR YOU

Matthew 15:21-28

It's true that you can count on Jesus in all things. You can count on Him even when He seems silent in your life. You can count on Him when things seem to be in disarray. You can count on Him even when His Word seems difficult to receive or understand. Do you believe me?

That's the message of this great passage from Matthew 15. In these verses we see a woman who's at the end of her rope. She's a loving mother who has a very sick daughter. The Bible says that "her daughter was troubled by a demon." Now people don't talk like that much today and such a statement seems foreign to our so-called modern ears, but such trouble is still oh, so very real.

Let's say it plainly. There is evil in the world; there is sin and guilt in the world. Satan is a real foe and, when you mess with him, there are terrible consequences. No explanations were needed for the mother in our text. This mother had seen it with her own eyes and she was on a quest to find help for her little girl.

Now I'm sure she had tried everything to bring healing to her daughter. Her motherly love was sure, it was certain. It was as deep a love as this world itself could give, but it wasn't enough.

Yet there was hope. Jesus was close by. She had heard of His miracles. She had heard of His compassion and grace. Even more, she knew that He was the Son of David, the One who would bring mercy and peace into this world. Maybe she had heard things about Him, like we sing today:

> "Hail the heaven-born Prince of Peace, Hail the sun
> of righteousness! Light and Life to all He brings, risen
> with healing in His wings!"

But when she finally gets to Him, she receives at first silence, then the rebuke of the disciples, and even a harsh word from Jesus Himself. Where else is she to go?

Have you ever been in a situation or known a time in your life when you were at the end of your rope, the end of your strength? You know, the time when you had given it your very best effort and it still was not enough? And to make matters worse, the problem is so big and your failures so public that strangers scoff at you and even your friends begin to avoid you. Times like these leave us all wondering if God really cares about what we're going through. Where do we go then?

Take a lesson from the woman in this passage. She would advise you to go to Jesus alone! Let's dig into this passage:

> "Leaving that place, Jesus withdrew to the region of
> Tyre and Sidon. A Canaanite woman from that vicinity
> came to Him, crying out, 'Lord, Son of David, have
> mercy on me!' But Jesus did not answer her a word."

Think about it. One of the most powerful forces in the world today is the committed love of a mother. The Canaanite woman reminds us of this very thing. The love of a good mom is a pretty special thing. Having confidence that there is one person in this world who won't give up on you, who encourages you when you are down, or honors you when you are up—that kind of love can literally change things.

It's been said that George Washington—the great leader of the American Revolution and the first president of the United States who was known for his courage, sacrificial leadership, and faith—once said, "I owe it all to my mother." That's committed love!

The one word that epitomizes the actions of caring moms is love, especially love for their children. Someone once wrote: "Mothers write on the hearts of their children what the cruel hand of the world cannot erase." It's been estimated that by the time a child reaches age 18, a mother has expended some 18,000 hours of dedicated work on his or her behalf out of love … that's just what moms do.

A certain second-grade teacher humorously learned this one day at school. She was teaching some very simple principles of physics and the focus of a certain lesson was magnets. She carefully explained the basic principle of magnetic attraction and demonstrated it by using a magnet to pick up some small metal objects. That Friday, though, when she gave a test on lessons taught that week, one of the questions read: "My name has six letters and it starts with "M." I pick up things. What am I?" She was somewhat surprised when more than half of the class answered "Mom."

We see committed love in our text today, and much more. The love of the Canaanite woman was extraordinary. She was willing to do whatever it took for her daughter. It doesn't say exactly what had been done, but I'm sure she had tried everything in her power to bring healing and hope to her suffering child. She was willing to go wherever she needed to go, to talk to anyone who would listen, and she remained undeterred by criticism or resistance.

Can there be any greater love than this? Yes! And that's the point in this Bible passage. Her love, as great as it was, was not enough. Her daughter was suffering and there was nothing she could do. Healing was beyond her capability and beyond her control. It's at times like these it becomes ever so important for us to realize that for the deep spiritual, physical, and emotional issues of life, we need something greater than even a mother's love!

The Bible says that the world in which we live is sinful. And sin isn't merely an occasional false deed or misspoken word; it is the condition of rebellion and self-centeredness that leads to separation from God Himself. Even the pains of sickness, struggle, and death are merely its shadows.

In the face of such things, even our loving best is in need of repentance and forgiveness. We sing songs like "what the world needs now is love, sweet love" and yet we continually treat each other with contempt and disregard. We need something more than just our love. While we say we know the meaning of love, many of our relationships are as disposable as the world in which we live.

We're very much like the young man in love who walked into a photography studio with a picture of his girlfriend that he wanted duplicated. The owner of the store noticed the inscription on the back of the picture and asked, "Do you want this copied too?" "Yes," the young man answered. "Are you sure?" "Of course!" Well, it turns out that while the inscription read, "My dearest Tom, I love you with all my heart. I love you more and more each day. I will love you forever. I am yours for all eternity" it also contained this: "
P.S. If we ever break up, I want this picture back."

The truth of the matter is that the love of sinful human beings, even at its best, is not enough for the ravages of sin, death, and the demonic forces that rage throughout the world in which we live. Not the love of a girlfriend, not the love of a mother.

Now before you accuse me of selling the power of a mother's love short, let me point out that I'm not the only one saying this. The woman in the text is shouting it to all who would listen. At first, she shouts, "Son of David, have mercy on me." Then as she draws closer to Jesus and kneels before Him, she changes her request from that of a momentary "have mercy on me"—as in, "deal with this one situation"—to something more long-term. She literally says, "Jesus, continually be my help!"

As one who had sacrificed everything for her daughter, as one who had never gone to sleep or risen from slumber without these concerns on her heart and mind, she is the one telling us today that—

not only for her and for her daughter but for you and me, too—what is needed for those deep spiritual and emotional issues of life is something that only God Himself can provide.

This mom didn't need to be convinced that what was needed was something more than she could give. She didn't need to be preached at that there was sin and evil in the world. She knew that all too well. Even more importantly, she knew that what was ultimately needed was God's attention, God's mercy.

For God's mercy is God's love in action for each of us. And that's the only kind of love that can heal. It can forgive; it can drive out the demonic; it can give courage in the midst of struggle; it can even deliver resurrection from the dead. She wasn't looking for a philosophy or a new self-help guru or a temporary fix. She was looking for Jesus, the Son of David who came to seek and to save the lost.

That's precisely the point—today we live in a world still in need of a Savior. The woman in this passage points us to a greater resource than human love. It's the infinite mercy of God in the Person and work of Jesus Christ; He is God's love in action for her and for us. And when she cries out to Jesus, she does so because she knows who He is and what He can do.

The Canaanite woman knew that God's merciful love was standing right in front of her! She knelt before Him and said, "Lord, continue to be my help!" Yet when He replied, "It is not right to take the children's bread and toss it to their dogs," she countered with, "Yes, Lord, but even the house dogs eat the crumbs that fall from the masters' table." Jesus' answer? "Woman, you have great faith!"

Think about it. Here was this person who, according to some, was from the wrong side of town and the wrong gender to be taken seriously. To others, she was of the wrong race and not one of the Chosen People. Yet here she was, a woman who despite all that believed that Jesus would ultimately hear her plea and answer her! A woman who even in the face of Jesus' puzzling conversation with her, still trusted in Him alone!

And what about Jesus' response? He seems to put her off, to even mildly insult her. Why would He do such a thing? It seems so unlike Him. Some say it was to deepen her faith and trust. I say it was to exhibit her faith, to demonstrate her faith for all to see! Her faith was a shining example, not only for those present but also for us today. She was basically saying, "Whatever You do for me, Jesus, it will be the best. I can put my trust in You alone. So, I'm committing my life, my daughter's life, to You. Period."

Faith is confident trust in Jesus Christ, no matter how things seem. Jesus draws such confident trust out of her so that all of us can see that faith in Him is sure! You can count on Jesus in all things! You can count on Him even when He seems silent. You can count on Him when things seem to be in disarray. You can count on Him even when His Word seems difficult to handle. Her humble faith demonstrates the confidence that Jesus would do what was best for her, no matter what.

Some might think that the woman's faith caused Jesus to act. But that misses the whole point! She knew the depth of the mercy of this Jesus who stood before her. He was the One whom David longed to see. He was the One whom Abraham, and Isaac, and Jacob yearned for. He was the Lord, the Master who brings God's mercy to her and to all.

She demonstrates this in her bold response as she states, "Lord, I have a master who treats me with mercy! You call me a house dog and I'm okay with that because it means I'm a part of Your house. You are my Lord, I'm with You. I'm no stray; I'm not on my own. I'm with You and that's all right!"

It may seem odd, but everyone in the world has a master. Most people go searching for love and peace and happiness in other sinful people or in inanimate things. They try to go it on their own, but what they don't realize is that Jesus' crumbs are better than everyone else's filet mignon. This Canaanite woman was saying, "Lord, if only Your crumbs … that's enough for me. If only Your loving touch … I will rest secure. If only Your simple word … I will be satisfied."

I wish I could have seen Jesus' face. He couldn't wait to bless her trust in Him. Jesus was overjoyed at such confidence in Him. He loves to help His people, to forgive them, to restore them. And through the lives of His believers, Jesus loves to make it known to the world that He isn't merely another solution. He isn't just another helper. He isn't just another problem solver. He is the One with mercy in His hands and eternal life in His wings!

It's hard to believe that there could ever be a greater love than that of the woman in our text. She had spent years of dedicated service to the needs of her daughter. She had exhausted every remedy and taken care of the one she loved in the most dire of circumstances. What love could be greater than this?

The Bible speaks of an infinitely greater love. One that not only loves friends and family, but even sinners and enemies. One that lives, and dies, and rises so that others might have real life and salvation. It's the love of God in Jesus Christ, God's mercy for the world in need. It is, in fact, the love that makes all those other loves possible.

His is a merciful love that left the comforts of heaven for you. His is a persevering love that walked this earth for you—to suffer the penalties of our sin for you, to endure the scoffing of His enemies and the rejection of His friends, to literally suffer the pains of hell in our place on the cross of Calvary—so that, with sin paid for and justice appeased, we all might be reconciled to Him again and have life and salvation in Him forever.

The cross and the resurrection of Jesus Christ is God's ultimate answer to the struggles we all face in this life. In his book *Outrageous Mercy*, author William Farley writes: "The Cross is our teacher. The cross is a window through which we learn everything we need to know about God, humanity, wisdom, worship, the purpose of suffering, the purpose of life, and a host of other issues. If you knew nothing else but the cross, but you knew it thoroughly, you would know everything essential for this life and the next."

Because of Jesus' work on the cross and His rising from the dead for you, the Bible says that you can count on Jesus when He seems silent. Even then He is at work for you and for those whom you love. You can count on Him when the world casts its ridicule on you. Even then, take heart that it is only momentary for He has overcome the world. You can count on Him when His Word seems hard to understand, knowing that in the struggles of life such exposed faith can be a blessing for those who see it in action.

If the little girl in this Bible account heard about all that her mother had done for her, how do you think she felt? Did such knowledge change her life? Even more, how about the mom and daughter? How did they feel when they heard about all the things that Jesus had done for them on the cross?

Jesus Christ, by the power of His Spirit, is inviting you to have faith like this Canaanite woman. It doesn't matter where you come from; it doesn't matter where you have been. He is calling you to Himself, to put your faith in Him, to come to His table. Not to receive scraps, but to receive His very best—His forgiveness, His life, His salvation for you. And to live in the strength and hope that only His mercy can provide.

While having a parent's love is important in this world, the deep, spiritual, emotional, even physical issues of life need more. We need God's mercy. We need His love in action for us.

Resurrection Reflections

1. What new insights did the Holy Spirit bring to your mind and heart as you read this chapter?

2. When have you ever found yourself at the mercy of others? How did that feel? How does it compare to receiving the mercy of Christ?

3. We have all sinned and fallen short of the glory of God. How then is it possible for us to be on the receiving end of God's mercy and grace?

4. It's been said that mercy is not getting what we deserve and that grace is getting what we don't deserve. Think of a time when the depth of God's mercy and grace was particularly meaningful. How would you describe that experience to others?

5. How did the faith of the Canaanite woman translate into action? In what ways can your faith be translated into action today?

CHAPTER FOUR

WE NEED A SHEPHERD

John 10:1-10

We need a Shepherd today. The world needs a Good Shepherd today.

That doesn't sound right, does it? I mean, we might say we need a financial planner. Or maybe a physical trainer or a personal therapist. We might even need a business coach, but I don't know too many people whose first thought is that they need a shepherd. How about you? Do you realize your need for Jesus, the Good Shepherd, today?

In the middle of WW I, an unexpected ceasefire peace broke out. It was Christmas Eve, December 24, 1914. The truce between the Germans and the British troops started when German troops began singing "Silent Night" ("Stille Nacht") just as the sun was going down. While they sang, they decorated the trees around their foxholes with candlelight. As the song pierced the air, the British troops were moved and began singing carols of the birth of Christ, too. As the evening progressed, people became more bold in their show of Christmas cheer. Christmas greetings began to be shared across enemy lines; some even became more bold, crossing no-man's-land to bring presents to their enemies. The rejoicing went on; the celebration continued through the night and on into Christmas Day.

Now, I must admit that while I had heard this story before, what I hadn't heard amazed me. As the ad hoc Christmas ceasefire took hold, each side also made a point of caring for the soldiers who had died in the previous day's battles. Funerals and proper burials were organized for both sides and—here it comes, this is what amazed me—a common song went up among both the German and the British troops. The song? "The Lord is my Shepherd, I shall not want. He makes me down to lie in pastures green, He leadeth me to quiet waters by."

The Good Shepherd-filled truce continued to spread across other lines, into other foxholes and trenches. Soon the whole war machine was at a standstill. There were even rumors of soccer games breaking out amongst those who just days earlier were firing bullets to kill. In some places, they say the truce lasted right up to New Year's Day. Unfortunately, new troops and new orders eventually broke the peace. The next year, commanders ordered the troops to bomb each other on Christmas Eve to make sure that such a peace didn't break out again.

Now, I'm not so naïve as to believe that we don't need policemen, soldiers, generals, or politicians. They exist in a sinful world to keep all hell from breaking loose. And I'm glad when they do the hard work that prevents that from happening. But, what that peace happen? What caused those enemies to see, even just for a moment, that they were brothers? It wasn't their nationality, or their economic standing, or even their persuasive personalities. They barely possessed the clothes on their backs, and they were probably more afraid than fearless.

The power of that peace was the Prince of Peace, the Prince of Peace who bonded enemies together, even for a moment, as sons of God. The Good Shepherd and His voice—His call to His people helped overcome real enmity, real hatred.

We need a Shepherd in this world. Someone to lead us back to God, to bond us again as brothers and sisters in Him. We need a Shepherd, One who not only keeps all hell from breaking loose, but One who can give us God's abundant life, One who can truly lead us even to heaven itself. We need a Shepherd to show us again what it means to be truly human, created and redeemed of God for others.

Listen to Jesus as He speaks in John chapter 10: "The man who enters by the gate is the shepherd of the sheep. The watchman opens the gate for him, and the sheep listen to his voice. He calls his own by name and leads them out … I am the Good Shepherd" (vs. 2-3, 11).

The Bible is clear. All people in this world need the Good Shepherd because we're like sheep who've gone astray. Jesus says this even more clearly when He calls all sheep to Him as the Good Shepherd. He says, in essence, "You not only need Me because you are lost; you need Me because there are literally forces out there seeking your destruction." Lost sheep are vulnerable to thieves and robbers. They need protection, they need to be saved, they need to be blessed and led. They need a Shepherd.

But, amazingly, that's the one thing people don't think they need today. They often think that just a bit more money will solve the problem; maybe just the loss of a few pounds, or maybe just a little common-sense advice, and we can handle the rest.

If you don't feel your *sheepness*, your lostness from God, then let the voice of God's Ten Commandments have its say with you today. Just try to find your way home to God by following these straightforward commandments, honestly and completely, in thought, word, and deed, 100 percent of every minute of every day. Just try to love your spouse, your friend, your neighbor, even your enemy, the way that Jesus loves you, at all times, in all circumstances. It won't take long to feel the weight of your inadequacies and failures. You'll sense pretty quickly that not only do you fail to measure up to God's standards, most of us don't even measure up to our own, because we are like sheep always going astray.

While it's embarrassing to think of oneself as a sheep, it is even more dangerous to deny one's *sheepness* and to live an un-shepherded life in this spiritually dangerous world. When sheep overconfidently go it alone, they are vulnerable to the wolf, the elements, and even their own inability to find their way home.

When I listen to some of the arrogant talk that exists in our world today, it sounds a lot like sheep talk. It sounds like people vulnerable to their own arrogance. When people say that the world just happened—

no God, morals, ethics, conscience, love, joy, peace … that it all just happened—that's sheep talk. When people say that there is no truth, that there is nothing really to guide us, that each one is in it for ourselves with no need for family, community, faith, religion—sheep talk!

Jesus tells us today one very important thing: Not only are we sheep who need a Shepherd, He is the Good Shepherd. He is the One who cares about us even more than we can care for ourselves. Yes, there is danger in this world; there is trouble in this world. But there is also a Shepherd in this world calling those who yearn for God's abundant life to follow Him! Trust in Him!

Listen as Jesus says, "The man who enters by the gate is the shepherd of the sheep. The watchman opens the gate for him, and the sheep listen to his voice. He calls his own by name and leads them out. I am the Good Shepherd!"

Then, let this Shepherd bless you today. Admit to yourselves that you are sheep in need of this Good Shepherd. All of us need to know, to admit, to believe, that we are not in this alone. The most powerful confession we can make today—whether we are a businessman or businesswoman, a husband, wife, or child, teacher, salesperson, president, king, queen or just a hard-working Joe or Josephine—is that all of us need the life and salvation that only God can give.

All of us need to know love and laughter, joy and victory over struggle. We need to know that Someone who really matters cares. We need Someone who has been through it all and can lead and guide us through this maze called life to the abundant life that only God can give! We need a Shepherd.

If you are spiritually or emotionally exhausted, having tried every way you know how to get a grip on life; if you have been run over by the kinds of struggles that tend to overwhelm us all; if you are someone who feels like there is no way you'll ever be able to overcome your past, let alone have hope for the future; if you know deep in your heart that you need a Shepherd, then good! You have a Shepherd, Jesus Christ. Trust in Him!

Jesus is bold to all who confess their need for Him; He is bold in His Word to you. He alone is the Good Shepherd. He doesn't just claim to be "a" Shepherd; He claims to be "the" Shepherd—the Good Shepherd you can trust, the One you can follow.

He is the Good Shepherd because He comes straight at you with His blessing; He comes right through the gate, just as He says.

I believe Jesus is saying, "Check Me out; I come straight through the gate for you. The watchman knows that I'm the real deal. Hear Me clearly; hear what I'm offering to you." Jesus doesn't try to trick you or fake you out; He doesn't sell you an inflated product! That's what the false shepherds do. He's the real deal.

It's like when I try to make an important purchase. I don't care if it's a car, a house, or a pair of shoes. I want to deal with someone who talks straight to me, who answers the questions I have because they're trying to really help me. I hate it when I'm dealing with sales people who won't answer my questions, don't you? You know, when you ask a specific question and they give an answer that has nothing to do with what you just asked? Their answers avoid the problems and merely highlight the benefits you already know. I don't trust anyone who won't deal with me in a straightforward manner.

Jesus says, then trust Me! I come right through the gate. I'm not like those who come over the walls, or come in the back way. They come to harm; I come to bless you, to forgive you, to call you home. Today I say, entrust your life to the Good Shepherd. He comes boldly, clearly, straight through the gate for you. But it's not just His manner that's key, it's also His message. He comes with His love—persevering, merciful love that He wants you to know and to trust.

In the prologue to his book *Leadership Jazz,* author Max Dupree writes about his granddaughter Zoe and the love she needed not just to survive, but to live. He writes, "Zoe was born prematurely; she weighed only 1 lb, 7 oz. She was so small that my wedding ring could slide up her arm all the way to her shoulder. The neonatologist who first examined her told us that she had a 5-10% chance of living merely three days.

When Esther and I saw Zoe in her Isolette in that neonatal intensive care unit, she had two IVs in her navel, one in her foot, a monitor on each side of her chest and a respirator tube and feeding tube in her mouth. To complicate matters, Zoe's biological father had jumped ship the month before Zoe was born. Realizing this, a wise and caring nurse name Ruth gave me these instructions: 'For the next several months, at least, you are the surrogate father.' She said, 'I want you to come to the hospital to visit Zoe. I want you to rub her body and her legs and caress her with the tips of your fingers, and while you are caressing her, tell her over and over again how much you love her because she has to be able to connect your voice to your touch.'"

Dupree came to the hospital every day and spent time with Zoe, not only to help her survive, but to help her begin to live, to make those cells grow and to help her heart grow, too. She needed more than just food and water; she needed the real, tangible love of a father. She needed a father who would dedicate his life to bringing a healing voice to her daily so that her body would begin to grow and mature.

We need God's love and mercy that way, too. We need Him in all things so that we can grow to be what He intended us to be. We need His healing touch. We need His loving voice to bless us. As sheep, we need the care of the Good Shepherd who brings the healing voice of God to us today. We need a Shepherd; we have a Shepherd—Jesus Christ!

Jesus is the Good Shepherd who also knows you by name. In the Near East, sheep were often given names, they were like family. Now, I don't know about you, but I wouldn't call sleeping with sheep the highlight of the shepherd's job! But, if I'm a sheep, I sure would want a shepherd like that!

Our Good Shepherd is right there where the sheep need Him to be, no matter what the cost. He doesn't bark orders from afar. He gets right in the middle of our lives, no matter how messed up they are at the moment, no matter how foul the smell, no matter how difficult the struggle. He comes right there to lead us out to abundant life! And the news gets greater still. He doesn't just "get in the mix" of our lives;

He is willing to lay down His life so that God's abundant life might be ours, as a gift.

Just think about what Jesus is saying to you. He's saying that this is how God comes to love you and care for you, to redeem you and call you home. Most people wouldn't risk their lives for insignificant sheep, and many people, sadly, wouldn't even give their lives for a fellow human being. But Jesus, God in human flesh, is not only willing to give His life for wayward sheep, this Good Shepherd literally gave His life on the cross so that you could be brought back into the fold of God's grace. Trust in Him!

Jesus is the Good Shepherd and He is calling you to follow Him today. You can trust Him amidst danger; you can be confident of His continued care; you can trust Him when He says that He can lead you to green pastures, quiet waters, and abundant life. He's calling you to follow Him because He has made the way for you already, as only the Good Shepherd can do.

He's made a way for life for you, no matter what you're facing today. If there is fear, He's faced it; a temptation, He's overcome it; real rejection, He's endured it; intimidation, threats, He's stood them down. He's literally overcome the gates of hell for you so that you might have life in Him. Only the Good Shepherd can do that. He's calling you to follow Him, to trust the path that He has fashioned for your life in Him.

When sheep successfully follow a shepherd through difficult terrain or through dangerous territory, you'll often see the hoofprint of the sheep in the middle of the footprint of the shepherd. When a wise, courageous, loving shepherd is leading the way, trusting sheep will follow his every move for their very lives. That's the way it is with Jesus, our Good Shepherd—our footprints in His no matter what the circumstance.

Remember that Christmas truce of 1914? How could such peace break out amongst enemies? It broke out because there was a Shepherd greater than their fears. Armies can win wars, but only the Good Shepherd and the bond of His grace can truly win the peace. They had a common bond that overcame their fears; they followed a common voice that bonded them beyond the terror and the gruesomeness of the moment. They knew a common Shepherd. Each one of them knew His promises: "Beneath Me, green pastures; beside Me, still waters. My Shepherd before me, a table around me, mine enemies after me, goodness and mercy beyond me—the house of the Lord."

We need that kind of Shepherd, that kind of life, and it's here for you today in Jesus Christ. Put your trust in Him and know that this Shepherd lives to protect and bless you. This Shepherd knows you by name and cares about you deeply. This Shepherd pursues you with His grace and calls you to follow in His mercy footsteps to live life abundantly for others in His Name!

Resurrection Reflections

1. What new insights did the Holy Spirit bring to your mind and heart as you read this chapter?

2. Be honest. Do you think you need a Shepherd? How? Do you find it easy or difficult to follow the Good Shepherd? Why?

3. We learn in this text that the Good Shepherd knows us and calls us by name. That means He knows us intimately. In what ways might knowing this make you uncomfortable? How might it bring you peace?

4. How would you describe feeling safe in the care of Christ, our Good Shepherd?

5. What role do faith and gratitude play in placing trust in Christ as our Good Shepherd?

CHAPTER FIVE

THE POWER OF A PERSEVERING FAITH IN JESUS

Philippians 3:8-14

It was July 4th, 1952. Florence Chadwick, aged 34, waded into the water off Catalina Island and began her 21-mile swim toward the coast of Southern California. If she completed her journey, she would be the first woman ever to accomplish this incredible feat. The water was icy cold and the fog was heavy, so much so that Florence could hardly see the boats in her own party. Sharks started to cruise her way as she swam. In surrounding boats, it took men armed with rifles, shooting carefully aimed shots to keep those sharks at bay.

Her most challenging enemy was not the sharks, but the constant, numbing cold of the water and the haze of the fog. Fifteen hours after she began, she dejectedly asked to be taken out of the water. Her muscles were now sluggish and unresponsive as the icy cold had finally taken its toll. Her mother and trainer, both alongside in the boat, kept trying to encourage her not to stop. They said, "We're near land; you've almost made it." But to no avail.

Chadwick looked ahead and all she could see was the dense fog, so she gave up. She was beaten and asked to be taken out of the water. When they pulled her out, incredibly, she was only a half-mile from the California coast! Only a small fraction of her journey was incomplete … she had almost done it! Later, when Florence's body began to thaw, the shock of her failure finally hit her. To a reporter she blurted, "Look, I'm not excusing myself. But if I could have just seen the land, I might have made it."

We, as a people, love to watch the daredevil or listen to the expert or the guru who has "accomplished something great." We muse that maybe, just maybe, their success might somehow become ours. But there always seems to be that eventual fog. In the end, there always seems to be something insurmountable. Even the present, great feats of strength, the great accomplishments of leadership and risk, eventually fade into history ... fade into the past.

In the book of Philippians the apostle Paul shares with us the power of a persevering faith in Jesus Christ—a faith in full view of such challenges, a faith that moves boldly into the future, that never fades into the past. Right up front he dismisses his and our capabilities as the reason for such power. Paul does not boast of himself, his abilities, his status, or his authority. His capabilities are useless compared to the power of knowing Jesus.

He speaks very simply of the power and victory of the Christian life in one word—faith. A persevering faith, not in oneself, or one's natural abilities, but a faith relationship to a living God who gives life and salvation to all who believe! Paul says, "Not that I have obtained this already, or have already been made perfect, but I press on to take hold of that which Jesus Christ has already laid hold of me" (vs. 12).

The power of a persevering faith, the power to "press on" in life is, first of all, the ability to know what is really valuable in life! Consider this ... if you have a faith relationship with Jesus Christ, then you have a new sense of what is truly precious! Paul says it this way in Philippians: "I consider everything a loss, compared to the surpassing greatness of knowing Jesus Christ as my Lord" (vs. 8).

Once you know this Jesus Christ—the One who is literally God in the flesh for you, the One who lived for you and died for you and rose so that you might have eternal life in His Name—what in the world can even compare? Paul says, "Nothing, nothing can even come close."

And knowing this Lord Jesus as your Savior by faith gives a person what I like to call the "power of no delusions and even greater expectations!"

Let me explain. Most people are either too hard or too easy on themselves. Christ says, "Be honest with yourself." When you trust in Him, then you let Him have His say in your life. The life of faith in Jesus means that you can be honest with yourself. It is the power of no delusions. When you realize that even your best efforts will not be enough—when you realize that your sin and failure are always with you, that there is no righteousness here on your own—Christ Jesus is already there with a forgiveness that only He can provide, with a love that only He can deliver and sustain.

But such honesty provides even greater news. By faith, His expectations are now yours as well. No delusions? Yes, but even greater expectations. Why? Because, by faith, the power of Jesus' resurrection, the accomplished purpose of His suffering and death, and the very hope of His future are yours and mine as well, just as He promises!

No delusions, even greater expectations—that's the power of faith in Jesus Christ for your life and for mine. That's the power to face life today and to press on to tomorrow, no matter what. Let's say it even more clearly: The power of such a persevering faith rests in knowing that there is one thing in life more important than everything else … faith in this Jesus Christ.

To persevere … someone once said that it means "doing the hard work, no matter what the obstacles, until the job is done." But I like this explanation more: To persevere is to "put your next foot forward, even though you don't have the strength to take another step."

What gives people the strength to persevere? What makes a person rise up to do his or her best when facing overwhelming odds and insurmountable obstacles? We value people who persevere because it gives us a glimpse of what humanity might be if we could somehow give it better than our best. We often value people who have faith in themselves for they are people who accomplish great things … at least compared to us. But there is temptation in such honoring.

Do you remember the Michael Jordan commercial of several years ago? Jordan was considered the greatest "winner" in basketball history and the Nike commercial went something like this: "I've missed more than 9,000 shots in my career. I've lost almost 300 games. Twenty-six times I've been trusted to take the game-winning shot and missed. I've failed over and over and over again in my life. And that is why I succeed."

He certainly put one foot forward when most everyone else couldn't take the next step. But if you asked Michael Jordan why he succeeded, I'm sure that he'd tell you it was because he had faith in himself, as most great athletes or leaders do. Now I'm not denying that such faith can do some pretty amazing things—it can cause people to set records swimming icy oceans, it can cause others to hit game-winning shots—but, in the end, it's not enough.

That's not the kind of faith we're talking about in Paul's letter to the Philippians. The kind of persevering faith that the world needs right now is not one rooted in our heroes' best efforts. This world of sin and suffering needs a greater source and resource for life and salvation than we can provide. The source of a persevering faith for real life and salvation can only come from God Himself; nothing else compares.

On the cross and in His resurrection from the dead, Jesus put one foot forward when no one else could take another step. And He didn't do it to show His greatness; He didn't do it to make a name for Himself. He did it because He loves you and He wants a life for you that only He can provide.

In the book *Through the Valley of the Kwai* by Ernest Gordon, an Allied prisoner of war, we get a glimpse of such a persevering love:

> The day's work had ended. The tools were being
> counted as usual. As the party was about to be
> dismissed, the guard shouted that a shovel was missing.
> The guard insisted that someone had stolen it, and of
> course this was a very serious offense because one may
> have used it to attempt an escape.

Striding up and down the ranks of men, the guard ranted and raved, working himself into a fury. Screaming in broken English, he demanded that the guilty one step forward to take his punishment. No one moved. The guard's rage reached new heights of violence.

"Then all die; all die," he shrieked.

To show he meant what he said, he cocked his rifle, put it on his shoulder, aimed at the first man in the rank, and prepared to shoot and work his way down the line. At that moment, a soldier from the Argyle Regiment stepped forward, stood stiffly to attention and said calmly, "I did it."

The guard unleashed all of his whipped-up hate, kicking the helpless prisoner and beating him with his fists. Still the Argyle stood rigidly to attention, chin up, though now blood was streaming down his face. His calm silence seemed to goad the guard's rage. Seizing the rifle by the barrel, the guard lifted it high over his head and brought it down upon the skull of the Argyle who fell limply to the ground, never to move again. And though it was perfectly clear that the man was dead, the guard continued to beat him and stopped only when he was exhausted.

The men of the work detail picked up their comrade's body and marched back to camp. When the tools were recounted again at the guard house, it turned out that the shovel was not missing after all.

Taking that sacrificial step forward for others, that's a glimpse of real love. On the cross we see it even more fully when Jesus put God's foot of eternal life and salvation forward for the whole world, not just for a few in the camp. Under the very curse of sin and death, with justice shrieking that all would deservedly die, Jesus put His saving foot forward so that all of us might live by His gracious, loving sacrifice. Jesus did it not only for comrades and friends, but even for enemies. He did it for you and He did it for me.

Paul knew this. He believed this and it changed his life. Knowing Christ by faith is the one thing that empowers a persevering life of faith.

As St. Paul writes, "Not that I have already obtained all this, or have already been made perfect, but I press on to take hold of that which Jesus Christ has already laid hold of me." Therefore, with the power of a persevering faith in Jesus, you can face whatever comes in this life in the knowledge of the victory that is yours in Him—because in Him there is power to forget what is behind.

Most of us tend to live in the past, and we're quite afraid of the future. We often romanticize what was and fearfully exaggerate what might be! In Christ, you can deal with where you have been. All the sin and guilt that you are carrying, all the weight of failed or unrealized expectations, all those things can be set aside because of Him. Your life is His. Your sins are forgiven in His Name, and you have a life to live because He seeks to live in and through you for others.

One of my favorite verses in the Bible is Ephesians 2:8-10 where Paul says that we are saved by grace through faith in Jesus. But then He also says that we are God's workmanship, created by Him to do good works that He has already prepared for us. What does that mean for you today? Well, no matter where you've been or what you've done, it can all be set aside because of Christ's sacrifice for you on the cross. It means that today you can start living the life He has prepared for you to live, a life that will not only leave the past in the dust, but one that will live boldly into His future.

With the power of a persevering faith in Jesus, you can face whatever comes in this life. Because in Him, there is power to strive toward what's ahead. You see, most of us are afraid of the future because the fear of the unknown incapacitates us. As we get older, the fogginess of the future becomes more and more apparent. But the power of faith in Jesus Christ says, "Of course, that's going to happen. What did you think? Are your skills and abilities your source of strength to face tomorrow, or am I?"

The term "press on" can give the wrong impression because it implies that Jesus has shown us the way and now we can simply roll up our sleeves and follow His example. It's as if He is our hero only, not our Lord and Savior. But the actual word used in the text is clearer than that; it could be translated "follow on." I like this translation better, because there we see Jesus "blazing the trail before us," overcoming obstacles that would overwhelm us and giving us a path to follow in Him for others, a life to live boldly now and forever.

"Follow on" because the One who has put His foot forward for you now empowers you to take another step in Him. "Follow on" in serving others in His Name, loving them with His resource of forgiveness, life, and salvation—something you've received, something that you cannot extinguish or exhaust.

How would you picture the kind of determined life of faith in Him that empowers you to face whatever you're dealing with today? It's as if Jesus is doing all things necessary so that you and I might live the life that He wants for us. It's as if there is no stopping Him in His blessing us, no matter what we are facing at any given moment.

This reminds me of a story about a father trying to teach his son how to hit a baseball. The trouble was that the boy was a bit too small and he hadn't practiced enough to hit the ball consistently. So dad did what dads do—he got out there and pitched the ball to his son again and again and again. The dad pitched, the boy missed; the dad pitched again, the boy missed. This went on several times.

The boy started swinging more slowly, then finally, half-heartedly. Sensing discouragement and trying to instill determination and not a quitter's attitude, the dad interjected, "Son, it's your responsibility to watch the ball and swing as hard as you can. It's my responsibility to hit the bat with the ball!" After an afternoon of determined swinging, his son said, "Dad, let's work on this tomorrow, okay? You're still missing my bat too much."

All of us will experience failure. Determination through a persevering faith is knowing that God's promises in our life will always hit, will always win out in the end! Press on and follow on, because your Savior has done all things necessary for your life and salvation, now and forever.

Remember Florence Chadwick, the one who tried to swim the Catalina Channel, the one who gave up because of the fog, the one who said, "If I could have just seen the land, I might have made it"? Two months after her failure, Chadwick walked off the same beach into the same channel and swam the distance, setting a new speed record, because this time she could see the land.

In the same way, the cross and resurrection of Jesus Christ cut through the fog, helping us see the certainty of what lies ahead for all who trust in Jesus. Such a faith gives us the power to overcome our past, the power to face the future, the power to persevere and live life boldly today and forever so others might know Him, too. The most exciting thing about being a Christian is the daily, even eternal, wonder of what Jesus can do with us as we live our lives by faith in Him. My prayer for you is that the power of a persevering, "follow-on" faith be yours, today and forever!

Resurrection Reflections

1. What new insights did the Holy Spirit bring to your mind and heart as you read this chapter?

2. What defeats have you experienced? When was a time you could only see the fog in front of you?

3. What things do you find yourself valuing over and above Christ? Where can you look to find the power and strength to value Christ over and above things?

4. What things are hindering your focus on Christ today? What do you need to forget that is behind? Work through that exists today? Press toward for the future?

5. In Ephesians 2:8-10 we are reminded that we are saved purely and simply by God's grace through faith in Jesus. What role then does faith play? Is it a response to God's great gift or the path to salvation itself?

CHAPTER SIX

WHAT'S PRECIOUS, HOLDS

1 John 1:1-13

In the movie *Castaway* Tom Hanks plays a character named Chuck Noland who works at FedEx. His job is to travel the world resolving productivity problems at various depots. On an ill-timed Christmas trip to Malaysia, while flying through a violent storm, his airplane crashes into the Pacific Ocean. He clings to life, floating in the middle of the ocean on a life raft. He finally washes up alive, though exhausted, on a deserted island.

For four years, he survives all alone on that island in the middle of nowhere. After years of unsuccessful attempts to escape, miraculously a gift of a makeshift sail washes up on shore, and he is finally able to make it out to sea. Even there, he almost dies, but somehow drifts into international shipping lanes, finally to be discovered by an ocean liner sailing back to America. Chuck can now actually get back to Kelly—the "love of his life"—and the life he once lived.

But, it's at this point, I think, that the real human drama begins. For upon returning to civilization, Chuck learns that he has long since been given up for dead. His family and friends held a funeral and Kelly worked through her grief and remarried. She now has a daughter with her new husband. The most dramatic scene in the movie is when Kelly receives a phone call and can't believe the voice on the other end. She answers, listens for a moment, and then faints, falling to the floor. Chuck is alive! Hearing his voice was overwhelming, but seeing him was almost too much to bear. There he was, right there. Chuck, the one whom she thought was dead, was alive. She could see him, touch him, hear him, even kiss him again. Hard to believe, but true.

Can you imagine the emotion of that reality? Can you even fathom the joy in the midst of that wonder? Well, that's merely a glimpse of the emotion in our Bible text for today. The apostle John—one who literally walked with Jesus, sat at His feet, listened to His voice—writes to this church back in the first century. Even more importantly, John writes to us, too, telling us about this Jesus who is unique in all the world. He was not only a real man, He was "God in the flesh." He was not just a teacher or a rabbi, He was the Word of Life, this world's only Lord and Savior.

This John—the last living apostle to witness the fullness of the life of Jesus face to face, literally in the flesh—writes this letter to encourage Christ's people in the world.

He writes to make his joy, their joy, complete (1:4) as they share their common faith in Jesus. He writes to warn Christians, then as well as now, about false teachings and false leaders who would deny the uniqueness of this Jesus and lead people away from the grace that only He could give (2:26). John writes to give us what he himself has received—eternal life (5:13) and fellowship with God the Father through His Son Jesus.

That's precisely what makes the beginning of this letter so unique. It is not a call to a unique piety. Lord knows, even now there are those who claim to have some new, secret, special plan to help us get our lives in order with their advice and our best efforts. There were already people in John's day saying they had a secret knowledge that went beyond Jesus, a really spiritual message that went beyond that of mangers, crosses, and Saviors who come in the flesh.

But John would have none of that. God's Good News from heaven was literally born into our flesh, walked this earth, lived our life, died our death, and gave us His mercy, His grace, His life, as a gift. God's Good News is about Him, about who He is for us and for all. John says, "That which was from the beginning, which we have heard, which we have seen with our eyes, which we have looked at and our hands have touched—this we proclaim concerning the Word of life" (vs. 1).

You might say that John was using a variety of ways to make sure we hear what he's saying about Jesus and His message for us. He talks about being in the presence of Jesus—but if we look at how he says it, it sounds rather crude in a somewhat down-to-earth way of speaking. Why? Because he wants us to know that, concerning God's life and salvation, this is as real as it gets. And this precious Good News of God is something we can truly, really receive.

Have you ever held something truly precious in your hands? That's usually one of those experiences you never forget—precious things you are able to touch and hold—things you able to bring near to your heart. Wow, that's very special!

Several years ago, my daughter visited her maternal grandfather. He was a veteran of WW II who had hit the beaches at Normandy. He brought her over to the case where he kept his medals from battle. He took them out, one by one, and placed them in her hands. As she held them gently in her hands, she saw history, right there before her eyes. She told me later that if her granddaddy were to leave her anything, she hoped it would be the one thing she would cherish most—a medal he had earned fighting for freedom, freedom that we enjoy today. Precious.

What would be that one thing for you? Maybe it's a special heirloom from your grandmother, grandfather, mom, or dad. Or maybe it's a special letter from the one you love—one that may have been written years ago but still speaks clearly of a love you can see in words, a love that's real because it's right there in your hands. Precious, wonderful!

Or maybe it's that newborn baby in a new mother's arms, or that newborn grandchild in granddaddy's hands. Now we're really talking precious, aren't we? A child that's been in its mother's womb for nine months—kicking, moving, and growing—but is now here, living and breathing on its own, yet still safe in its mother's arms. Or that grandfather whose heart is melting because he is literally seeing life from both ends. As one gets older, the real, precious things become even more magnified in their realness.

You don't just want to hold such things; you want to hold them dear! Such things are precious—the heirlooms and beloved trinkets that hold a special place on your mantle or a shelf in the living room. And the people who are precious in your life? You hold them dear in your heart.

But as truly great as all of these might be, the even greater good news of this text is that God holds you dear in His hands and in His heart, through the Person and work of Jesus. While John talks about having fellowship with fellow believers, this is no general talk about relationships. It's specific—God's offer to bond us together in the real Presence of His Son, our Savior.

Fellowship with God is real and it requires something spiritually tangible at the center, at the core—something from God Himself, something to hold us to Himself and to each other. It's not a fellowship of our common memories or our common emotions, no matter how powerful they might be. It's not even a fellowship of our common commitments. This is a fellowship that God Himself offers and creates in us and through us as we receive Him through common things like words, water, bread, and wine. It's a common receiving of the real, present Lord who forgives us each the same, who lives truly in us the same, and whose Spirit empowers us to be His people for others.

John is saying that's what's most precious, almost too much to be believed, is indeed true. Even in this modern world of brazen pride—where people often feel their problems can be solved at the altar of their best efforts and wisdom—there are yet those who yearn to know what true love is, what lasting peace is, what forgiveness can really be in their lives. I pray that you are one of those people yearning to know such truth, such good news.

That's why John says it so plainly: "We saw it, we lived it, we experienced it, we received it." God's love, mercy, grace, and peace has a Name—Jesus the Christ, who actually walked our walk, breathed our air, ate our food, and gave us His life!

In the title song from her album *Love Has a Name*, Kathy Troccoli says this so beautifully through music. You know, the great thing about music—about psalms, hymns, and spiritual songs—is that it expresses incredible Bible truths so beautifully and clearly, using the garment only music can bring. She sings it so well when she says:

"Love has a name, Love has a face
And when you know love, You know you're not the same.
Love never dies, Love never leaves
And when hope is gone, Love will believe.
Love every day, Give love away. Love has a name,
Love came from heaven, and died for us all.
Now we are forgiven by the Savior of the world,
the Savior of the world."

I think John would have loved it if someone would have put this text to music. I think he wouldn't have just said it, he would have sung it. "That which was from the beginning—which we have heard, which we have seen with our eyes, which we have looked at and which our hands have touched—this we proclaim concerning the Word of life. The life that appeared—we have seen it, testify to it, and we proclaim to you—is eternal life, which was with the Father and appeared to us. We proclaim to you what we have seen and heard, so that you may have fellowship with us. And this fellowship we share is with the Father and with His Son, Jesus Christ." (1 John 1:1-3)

So … be amazed anew with the apostle John today. In fact, why not read the whole letter? It's short, but powerful. With John, then, look, touch, and hold this incredible Messiah—Jesus—to yourself in faith. He is God in the flesh. He is the One who died, yet now He lives. He is the One who forgives, empowers, and blesses you as only He can.

Trust Him. Get to know Him through His Word. There is no Person like Him; there is no Savior like Him; there is no God like Him. Do you wish to know God? He wants to know you. Do you wish to find God? He wants to be found. He is a Savior who is coming to you today in the very words of this lesson so that you can know the One who wants to be known by you.

But, be careful here, my friend. Remember, the great apostle John isn't cajoling us to hold on to Jesus tighter. This isn't some moralistic call to be a more concerned Christian about the things of Jesus so that, hopefully, then and only then, will Jesus bless you.

No, this is a message proclaiming the utter joy of knowing that Jesus wishes to come to you through His gifts—gifts put into your hands, into your eyes, into your hearts and minds to bring you to the joy of faith. Gifts to bless you by the power of His Spirit, to give life, abundantly, now and forever.

In fact, the real power of the Christian life is to know that faith's power is the strength of His grip of grace, His hold on your life. Don't ever confuse the confidence that God wants you to have in your walk of faith with the power of our own decisions. Don't ever give in to the temptation to think that it has anything to do with the strength of your commitment to Him. For whether you are weak or whether you are strong, it is because of Jesus that you are the Lord's. Even growing up and maturing in your walk with Him is a daily call to remember the strength of His grip of grace, the power of His mercy in your life.

And sometimes it's really good to know that my grip isn't the key, isn't it? Sometimes I'm just thankful that I'm still hanging on—or better yet that He's got me even more strongly—when I feel weak and overwhelmed. It takes the pressure off, doesn't it, to know that our joy, our forgiveness, our peace is in His hands.

So with eyes that can read His Word; with a mind that can be led by His promises; with a mouth that can taste His grace in His supper; and with a confidence that He holds on to me by the power of His Spirit, I can strive to live life faithfully, boldly, even courageously, for His glory and for my neighbor's good. It's good to know that, as we grab hold of grace and try to live life in God's Spirit, even there the strength of our grip isn't the key!

Our light grip of faith, His sure grip of grace in action. That's the way to live life to its fullest. By God's grace, don't let go. Grab hold of life confidently, joyfully, and lightly. Don't grip too hard—like with a death grip or a vise grip—as if God were trying to somehow take it from you, even as He gives it to you. No, grip it confidently but lightly, because God's got a hold of you surely. And, to use a golf metaphor, "swing away!"

Such was the advice given to one of the greatest golfers of all time who, sadly, may never be recognized as such. Why? Because at the most dramatic moment of his career, he faltered. Greg Norman was one of the greatest golfers to have ever played the game. Early on, the swashbuckling star burst onto the golf scene from Australia with a game that many thought would land him someday in the same discussions as Nicklaus, Palmer, and Hogan. But that was not to be. Several times, freak things began to happen to him or against him in the final rounds of major tournaments. Finally, on one fateful day, he fell apart on the last round in one of the biggest tournaments of his life.

Jack Nicklaus, who many believe was the greatest golfer of all time, was rooting for Greg Norman to succeed. He noticed that, despite his talent, one thing continued to happen to him under pressure. That smooth, powerful swing was suddenly full of tension. So, before the final round at the Masters, Nicklaus was said to have told him, "Greg, don't grip the club so hard. Lighten your grip; let the club do its work." But, sadly, whether he couldn't or wouldn't, Norman's grip tightened that day and he lost it all.

The joy of our life in Jesus Christ is not the strength of our faith grip of His grace; it is the real, present grace grip of His message in our lives. Nicklaus may have urged Norman to lighten his grip so that the club could do its work; John would tell us today to lighten our grip so that the cross—the Word of Life, literally and truly in our lives—can do its work for us and through us to others.

John is proclaiming to you today a word of life for your life. But it's not merely a word on a page or a thought in our minds. This message is about a real Lord and Savior, one that John literally saw, touched, hugged, and held. He was precious in his hands. The greatest news of all is that Jesus came literally for John, to John. This Savior held on to him—preciously, graciously, mercifully, eternally—in words he could hear, in water in which he could be washed, and in bread and wine he could receive.

Let Jesus hold you today in the same way by His grace. Receive all that He has come to give you by faith because He—the Precious One, the unique Savior for the whole world—will never lose His grip on you! For that which is precious, holds!

Resurrection Reflections

1. What new insights did the Holy Spirit bring to your mind and heart as you read this chapter?

2. What heirloom do you want to pass on to the next generation? What are some ways you can pass the legacy of faith on to others?

3. Salvation is a gift granted to us through faith in Christ's victory over sin, death, and the power of the devil. When does it become tempting to think that salvation depends on our actions rather than God's?

4. Why is it essential to be in fellowship with other believers and to receive the means of grace—the tangible bestowing of Christ's forgiveness through Word and Sacrament?

5. How can remembering your baptismal covenant equip you for becoming God's blessing to others?

CHAPTER SEVEN

LIVING HOPE IN A DEAD HOPE WORLD

1 Peter 1:3-9

I love Easter Sunday. I love it when Christians greet one another with "Christ has risen!" And I love it when fellow Christians answer, "Christ has risen, indeed! Hallelujah!" Last Easter I was telling a friend that when sharing those words in church, I get goose bumps! Still today, those words bring a great big smile to my face!

There is really nothing quite like the thrill of celebrating Christ's victory over death and the grave on the great day of resurrection. For Christians, Easter is THE greatest day of the church year. In more ways than one, you might say that we LIVE for it! Churches are jam-packed. Choirs seem to hit all the high notes. People are especially joyful. No one wears a frown. The pleasure of the Gospel gladdens every heart and lightens every face because Easter is all about Jesus and what He did when He rose from the grave. This is a day of hope—LIVING hope.

It's kind of interesting, therefore, that one of the lowest attended services in the church year is actually the Sunday after Easter. Isn't that odd? You'd reason that after such a festive, wondrous Sunday as Easter that even more people would be back the next week. I suspect that in some congregations that may be true. Traditionally, though, that is not the case.

Maybe one of the reasons for the letdown is that the imprint of the world makes its mark on us. Within just a few days after Easter, the world that is dying all around can really start dragging us down. I mean, life is hard! Even the strongest of Christians can feel the weight of the world and their shoulders can start to slump. But that's what makes today's Bible passage so good and helpful. We need a Word that helps us with the letdowns in life.

The Word of the Lord for today comes from 1 Peter 1, beginning at verse 3: "Blessed be the God and Father of our Lord Jesus Christ! According to His great mercy, He has caused us to be born again to a living hope through the resurrection of Jesus Christ from the dead, to an inheritance that is imperishable, undefiled, and unfading, kept in heaven for you, who by God's power are being guarded through faith for a salvation ready to be revealed in the last time. In this you rejoice, though now for a little while, if necessary, you have been grieved by various trials, so that the tested genuineness of your faith—more precious than gold that perishes though it is tested by fire—may be found to result in praise and glory and honor at the revelation of Jesus Christ."

Let me remind you that Peter wasn't inspired by God to write this letter, first and foremost, to all of the people living in the United States, to us Christians who live in the quieter areas of rural America or the safer areas of our city suburbs. Peter was writing this word to Christians who were certain to suffer, or were already suffering, some pretty harsh persecutions by those who opposed the followers of Jesus.

It turns out that it's not just the Christians under the Roman rule of Nero who have suffered. Recently, The Center for Studies on New Religions reported that in 2016 some 90,000 Christians had lost their lives around the world because of persecution.[3] Such reports make Peter's letter relevant for Christians today. They also make our confession of the Christian faith relevant, our prayers important, and our hope in the resurrection a necessary testimony.

Christians are dying today because of their faith in the resurrection of Jesus Christ from the dead. My friends, do you ever feel that kind of heat, that kind of persecution for your beliefs? Maybe not to the same extreme, but you do feel persecution. You may know the loneliness of staying home from parties you weren't invited to, or the vulgar talk at work that makes you uncomfortable, or the pain of wanting to do your best only to have your salary cut by those who don't share your values or value you, a Christian.

What is it that causes you to willingly suffer scorn or injustice? What is it that makes Christians around the world today, living in regions of certain countries, so willing to die? Well, the answer is best found in the Word of God. Here Peter reminds Christians that their faith and life would be persecuted by others. He also reminds them of just who provides for their every need: "Blessed be the God and Father of our Lord Jesus Christ! According to His great mercy, He has caused us to be born again to a living hope through the resurrection of Jesus Christ from the dead, to an inheritance that is imperishable, undefiled, and unfading, kept in heaven for you" (vs. 3-4).

Any and all hope for you and me is a result of Jesus' death on the cross and His resurrection. The persecuted and dying Christians in Peter's day, and ours, testify to this: no matter how hard the world tries to steal your joy or your faith, you have an identity and an inheritance in Christ Jesus that can never be taken from you. This faith is a gift to you, not something earned because you were strong enough, good enough, suffered enough, or were faithful enough. The Bible says, "According to His great MERCY, He has caused us to be born again."

Mercy indicates that it is God's provision for you. More than that, it was Jesus who acted mercifully on your behalf and mine when He suffered the cruelty of crucifixion. Consider this: God demands a sacrifice for sin and sinfulness that was supposed to be our death. But Jesus took it instead. He died a death He didn't deserve to give us a gift we could never earn—an inheritance that can NEVER be taken away ... "kept in heaven FOR YOU"!

You may already know the story of Louie Zamperini, but let

me share a few insights. Louie was a World War II Prisoner of War who suffered tremendous cruelties in a Japanese prison camp after his Army-Air Force bomber crashed into the Pacific Ocean.[4] He was brutally treated for 27 months. After his release, Zamperini came back to the States and his life became a mess. Suffering from PTSD, he self-medicated with alcohol and picked fights with others. Even his wife said that it had gotten so bad she had threatened to divorce him, that is, until she heard the voice of God through the preaching of a Christian named Billy Graham.

Unlike his wife, Louie wasn't so easily impressed, and he walked away several times, especially when Graham tackled the subject of sin. Then one day, he heard this preacher say that people turn to God when they are at the end of their ropes and have nowhere else to turn.[5] The Gospel, the power of the resurrection, suddenly took hold. It breathed life into his worn-out and battered heart. This Word of Resurrection and Hope and New Life caused Louie to give up the drink and get high on Christ. It caused him to let go of his anger and forgive his captors. And it ultimately caused his entire life to change!

The Gospel breathes life into tired bones and struggling souls. Now, Zamperini's life wasn't all glorious after that revelation of grace and mercy and hope. He struggled with the trauma of his war experience; it would haunt him still. But the difference was found in this: it no longer controlled him. Louie was enabled, by the power of God's forgiveness, to live on a higher plain and forgive his captors. Listen for this kind of refrain any time you hear of Christians being persecuted or killed today. The follow-up news stories of such atrocities will often uncover persecuted Christians forgiving their adversaries. They oftentimes share the message of hope with their captors or executioners. It is truly amazing, but that's what it means to be born into a living hope! That's the power of the Gospel at work today!

Keep in mind that is not a message about Louis Zamperini or any others you may know. We would all be in trouble if we started to worry whether we had the same kind of strength and conviction as others. That would be unfair to them and to us. After all, that kind of strength does not rest in the arms of a human being, it rests in the Lord. You are "born again to a living hope through the resurrection of Jesus Christ from the dead" and further let me read, "to an inheritance that is imperishable, undefiled, and unfading, kept in heaven for you, who by God's power are being guarded through faith for a salvation ready to be revealed in the last time." Now that's solid.

Think about this: What investment in life provides you with a guarantee of anything that is imperishable, undefiled, or unfading? Who or what agency can guard your greatest cares or most cherished loved ones in such a permanent way? Let me help you out. The answer is NOTHING! In fact, whenever we try to guard our possessions from anyone or anything taking them from us, we are probably hanging on too tight. When our joy comes from the things of this life, we are prone to disappointment, and our hearts to being crushed. The objects of this kind of joy never last. And the objective of our lives is limited to this world only.

Kathy McCullough recently published *Ups and Downs*, an autobiography of her life as a former Northwest Airlines 747 captain. In it she shares the story of her struggle as a woman to reach and be accepted in the field of the elite in aviation.[6] Reading her story, you discover how there appeared to be so many more lows than highs, so many times when it would have been easier to quit rather than fight the personalities that wanted to keep her grounded.

Hers is a story of how the world forever seems to threaten our life, our work, and our achievements. In fact, upon reaching the pinnacle of her career, it wasn't crusty old guys who wanted to push her out; it was cancer that forced her into retirement. So, you see, you and I are not able to control or guard ourselves from the destructive nature of this world or the people who live for status in this world alone. But yours and mine is a living hope from a living Lord. It is what Captain McCullough shares that allowed her to strive and really live. God got her through the ranks in aviation and keeps her going still today.

No doubt your life has been one of many ups and downs. Life is fun when you're riding a high point, but even when life comes crashing down, it will not crush you. Why? How can you and I be so confident of this? Peter reminds us that we are IN Christ Jesus, and ours is a LIVING HOPE for a dying world. He says, "In this you rejoice, though now for a little while, if necessary, you have been grieved by various trials, so that the tested genuineness of your faith—more precious than gold that perishes though it is tested by fire—may be found to result in praise and glory and honor at the revelation of Jesus Christ" (1 Peter 1:6-7).

Expect trials to come your way. Maybe, expect tumultuous trials and griefs to come your way. But know that these are just battles. Remember, the victory in matters of life and death has been won already in Christ Jesus. Your life is golden, and your eternal inheritance has been made secure in Jesus' death and resurrection. Nothing can separate you from the love of God that is yours in Christ Jesus. Jesus secured your identity AND your inheritance! Now, your life—filled with ups and downs—is nothing less than a magnificent song of praise and glory and honor for God our Heavenly Father, at the revelation of Jesus Christ.

Resurrection Reflections

1. What new insights did the Holy Spirit bring to your mind and heart as you read this chapter?

2. Where do you see evidence that the world is in dire need of the hope that only Christ can bring?

3. What words would you use to describe what the culmination of Holy Week in Easter means to you?

4. How might you go about sharing the great good news about what Christ has done for you to someone who does not yet know Him as Lord and Savior?

5. What stirs hope in your heart as you face the challenges life brings until that day Christ calls you to Himself for all eternity?

ENDNOTES

1. LCEF employee

2. History vs. Hollywood, "SULLY (2016)" (History vs. Hollywood, 2016), http://www.historyvshollywood.com/reelfaces/sully/.

3. Thomas D. Williams, Ph.D., "Report: 90,000 Christians Killed for Their Faith in 2016" (*Breitbart*, January 1, 2017), http://www.breitbart.com/national-security/2017/01/01/report-90000-christians-killed-faith-2016/.

4. Laura Hillenbrand, *Unbroken* (New York: Random House, 2014).

5. Czarina Ong, "Louis Zamperini's son shares details of his father's faith that did not make it to Unbroken film" (*Christianity Today*, March 31, 2015), https://www.christiantoday.com/article/louis.zamperinis.son.shares.details.of.his.fathers.faith.that.did.not.make.it.to.unbroken.film/51085.htm.

6. Kathryn Anne McCullough, *Ups and Downs* (KMC Publishing, November 1, 2016).

Chapter One
Repentance Refreshment — Acts 3:18-21
#79-33
Presented on The Lutheran Hour on April 22, 2012

Chapter Two
Humble Strength for Eternal Salvation — Philippians 2:5-11
#84-32
Presented on The Lutheran Hour on April 9, 2017
By Rev. Dr. Gregory Seltz, Lutheran Hour Speaker

Chapter Three
Count On Christ's Mercy for You — Matthew 15:21-28
#78-35
Presented on The Lutheran Hour on May 8, 2011
By Rev. Dr. Gregory Seltz, Lutheran Hour Speaker

Chapter Four
We Need a Shepherd — John 10:1-10
#78-36
Presented on The Lutheran Hour on May 15, 2011
By Rev. Dr. Gregory Seltz, Lutheran Hour Speaker

Chapter Five
The Power of a Persevering Faith in Jesus — Philippians 3:8-14
#79-04
Presented on The Lutheran Hour on October 2, 2011
By Rev. Dr. Gregory Seltz, Lutheran Hour Speaker

Chapter Six
What's Precious, Holds — 1 John 1:1-13
#79-32
Presented on The Lutheran Hour on April 15, 2012
By Rev. Dr. Gregory Seltz, Lutheran Hour Speaker

Chapter Seven
Living Hope in a Dead Hope World — 1 Peter 1:3-9
#84-34
Presented on The Lutheran Hour on April 23, 2017
By Rev. Dr. Gregory Seltz, Lutheran Hour Speaker

50058290R00044

Made in the USA
Middletown, DE
24 June 2019